HOW TO FIND A JOB WITH LINKEDIN

Get the Job of Your Dreams.

Own your future.

LinkedIn is the world's biggest job market.

SW Prem Jaganu

TABLE OF CONTENTS

Introduction

Your Journey Begins Here

Welcome to a transformative journey that redefines your professional growth and job-hunting approach in the digital era. This book is not just a guide; it's a comprehensive roadmap to mastering LinkedIn, the world's most extensive professional network. Whether you are a mid-career professional feeling stagnant in your current role or a marketing expert with leadership aspirations, this guide caters to your unique career paths.

In today's dynamic job market, traditional job search methods are rapidly evolving, overtaken by the capabilities of online platforms, with LinkedIn at the forefront. It's a complex landscape offering a multitude of opportunities, connections, and resources for continuous career development. Job hunting has transformed from a passive activity to a proactive, strategic utilization of LinkedIn. This platform is your key differentiator, enabling you not just to seek jobs but to carve a fulfilling career aligned with your personal and professional goals.

This book will guide you through customizing your LinkedIn experience, reflecting your unique career story and objectives. It addresses challenges like the competitive job market, balancing career progression with personal commitments, overcoming gender biases, and keeping pace with digital evolution. You'll learn practical, actionable strategies that delve into the depths of LinkedIn's functionalities.

At its heart, LinkedIn is about building relationships and community. We explore authentic and effective networking, turning connections into opportunities and these opportunities into career milestones. Beyond optimizing your profile, the book delves into personal branding, content creation, understanding the recruiter's perspective, interview preparation, and negotiation mastery. LinkedIn is not just a tool but a catalyst for personal and professional transformation.

The journey with LinkedIn is continuous, focusing on learning, adapting, and growing. We'll show you how to maintain an ever-ascending career trajectory, utilizing LinkedIn Learning, staying updated with market trends, and future-proofing your career.

As we embark on this journey, remember this book is a companion in your quest for a fulfilling career. It's about thriving in a career that aligns with your ambitions and life's blueprint. Let's turn the page and step into a world of endless possibilities with LinkedIn.

The Power of LinkedIn in Today's Job Market

In a time when the professional world is constantly changing due to the digital landscape, LinkedIn stands as a beacon of opportunity and advancement. This introduction delves into the immense potential of LinkedIn, a platform that has revolutionized job hunting and career development in the 21st century. It's more than just a professional network; it's a multifaceted tool that opens doors to a world of possibilities.

For professionals across various stages of their careers, LinkedIn is the key to unlocking potential and navigating the complexities of today's job market. It's a platform where career paths are not just discovered but also carved and refined. From the IT professional eyeing a leap into upper management to the marketing expert aspiring to re-enter the workforce, LinkedIn serves as the common ground where ambitions meet opportunities.

The digitalization of the job market has made online networks like LinkedIn indispensable. It's where recruiters look for talent, where industry leaders share insights, and where job seekers find their next big opportunity. The strength of LinkedIn is found in its capacity to match people with opportunities that complement their qualifications, experience, and desired careers. This is about more than finding a new job. It's about finding the right job, the one that fits your vision of career success and personal fulfillment.

LinkedIn goes beyond conventional job-search techniques. It enables you to present your professional self, form deep connections, and keep up with market developments. For the modern professional, being on LinkedIn is not a choice but a necessity. It's where your digital footprint translates into real-world career advancements.

However, navigating LinkedIn has its challenges. It requires a strategic approach, one that understands the nuances of digital networking, personal branding, and online engagement. This book guides you through these complexities, offering practical advice and insights tailored to your unique career journey. Whether you're looking to climb the corporate ladder, pivot to a new industry, or balance professional growth with personal commitments, this book will show you how to leverage LinkedIn to your advantage.

As we embark on this journey, remember that LinkedIn is more than a platform; it's a community. It's a space where professionals from diverse backgrounds converge to share, learn, and grow. By mastering LinkedIn, you're not just enhancing your career prospects; you're becoming a part of a global professional community—a community that's constantly evolving, just like the job market itself.

In this book, we'll explore the transformative power of LinkedIn in today's job market. We'll provide you the know-how to successfully traverse this ever-changing platform, enabling you to forge lucrative and satisfying career paths. The journey begins now, and the path to professional excellence awaits.

CHAPTER 1

Understanding LinkedIn

The LinkedIn Landscape

In the vast expanse of the digital professional world, LinkedIn stands as a pivotal platform, a virtual crossroads where career paths intersect with opportunities. It's a landscape that continually evolves, adapting to the changing dynamics of the job market and the professional aspirations of its users. From the bustling hubs of major cities to the dynamic corridors of tech industries, LinkedIn's reach is expansive and inclusive, encompassing professionals from diverse backgrounds and career stages.

The realm of LinkedIn is a digital mirror of the professional world, reflecting the intricacies of career development, networking, and job hunting. Its topography is rich with features designed to foster professional growth, from the comprehensive profiles that serve as digital resumes to the intricate networking systems that connect millions of professionals across the globe. For the mid-career IT expert in New York or the emerging marketing leader in San Francisco, LinkedIn is the common denominator in their professional journeys.

At its core, LinkedIn is a multifaceted ecosystem teeming with recruiters, job seekers, thought leaders, and industry experts. It's a platform where the exchange of ideas, opportunities, and insights is not just facilitated but actively encouraged. In this landscape, your profile is your billboard, showcasing your skills, experience, and aspirations to a global audience.

The LinkedIn Landscape is not static; it's a vibrant, ever-changing environment that responds to the needs of its inhabitants. It's a place where new features emerge, such as LinkedIn Learning for continuous skill development or sophisticated job search functionalities that connect candidates with their ideal roles. These features are more than tools; they're bridges connecting ambition with reality and aspiration with achievement.

For the ambitious professional, LinkedIn is both a showcase and a tool. It's where personal brands are built and nurtured, where thought leadership is cultivated, and where meaningful professional relationships are forged. In this landscape, every connection, post, and interaction is a step towards a larger goal, be it career advancement, industry recognition, or work-life balance.

Navigating the LinkedIn landscape requires more than just a presence; it demands a strategy. It's about knowing how to make the most out of the tools on the platform, interact with your network, and optimize your profile. This chapter is your guide through the maze of LinkedIn's features, helping you to decode the nuances of digital networking and personal branding.

As we traverse this landscape, we'll explore the building blocks of a robust LinkedIn presence, from crafting a compelling profile to networking effectively and engaging with the platform's myriad features. You'll learn how to make LinkedIn work for you, whether you're seeking a job, exploring new career avenues, or simply looking to expand your professional network.

In the end, LinkedIn is more than just a social network; it's a catalyst for professional transformation. It's where careers are not just developed but also redefined. This chapter is your first step in mastering the LinkedIn landscape, laying the foundation for a journey that will reshape your professional destiny. Welcome to the world of LinkedIn, where every connection is a potential opportunity, and every interaction is a step towards your career goals.

Building Your Professional Identity

In the digital age, where your online presence often makes the first impression, crafting a professional identity on LinkedIn is akin to laying the foundation for your career's skyscraper. It's where your digital persona meets the professional world, a platform where the potential is visualized, and ambitions take a tangible form. This chapter is dedicated to guiding you through the art of sculpting your professional identity on LinkedIn, turning it into a magnet for opportunities and a reflection of your career aspirations.

Imagine LinkedIn as a vast, bustling city where every building represents a professional. Some skyscrapers soar high, radiating confidence and success, while others are still under construction, full of potential and ambition. Your task is to build your skyscraper - your professional identity - in this city. It's not just about stacking floors; it's about architectural design, the materials you use, and how your building complements the skyline.

Your LinkedIn profile is more than just a resume; it's a canvas where you paint your professional story. It's where your past experiences, current skills, and future aspirations converge. Each section of your profile - from your headline to your experience, endorsements, and accomplishments - is a stroke of paint on this canvas, collectively presenting a picture of who you are as a professional.

But how do you ensure your building - your profile - stands out in the skyline of LinkedIn? It starts with introspection and strategy. Understanding your unique value proposition is critical. Are you a seasoned IT professional with a knack for innovative solutions? Or a marketing maven with a flair for brand storytelling? Identifying your strengths and how they align with your career goals is the first step in constructing your LinkedIn profile.

As you build your profile, remember it's not just a list of jobs and qualifications. It's a narrative of your professional journey. Your summary section is your elevator pitch, a chance to captivate your audience with your passion, expertise, and vision. Your experience section is not just a timeline of roles; it's a chronicle of your growth, challenges, and achievements.

Networking on LinkedIn is like the intricate wiring that powers a skyscraper. It's about making connections that light up opportunities. But effective networking on LinkedIn is more than just adding contacts; it's about building relationships. Engaging with your network through thoughtful comments, sharing insights, and offering support make your presence on LinkedIn not just visible but valuable.

As you navigate through the chapters of this book, you'll learn how to refine each element of your LinkedIn profile. You'll discover how to make your headline captivating, your summary compelling, and your experience impactful. You'll understand the power of recommendations and how to showcase your skills effectively. This chapter lays the groundwork for your LinkedIn journey, helping you to build a profile that not only reflects your professional identity but also propels your career forward.

In the end, your LinkedIn profile is your billboard in the digital job market. It's what potential employers, recruiters, and colleagues see before they meet you. A well-crafted LinkedIn profile opens doors to opportunities, conversations, and career advancements. It's where your professional identity meets the world, where you tell your story and set the stage for your next career leap. Let's embark on this journey of building not just a LinkedIn profile but a professional identity that resonates with your aspirations and echoes your achievements.

Privacy and Settings

In the tapestry of your professional life, LinkedIn serves as both a window and a shield. It's where your professional identity meets the world, yet it's also a place that demands careful navigation through privacy and settings. This section of the book delves into the nuanced world of LinkedIn's privacy and settings, empowering you to take control of your online professional presence.

Imagine LinkedIn as a grand stage where your professional story unfolds. Just as in theater, where curtains and backdrops play crucial roles, LinkedIn's privacy and settings are the tools that allow you to control how much of your professional life is revealed and to whom. These settings are your backstage levers, ensuring that your professional narrative is shared with the right audience in the right way and at the right time.

Privacy on LinkedIn is about balance. It's about being visible to potential opportunities while safeguarding your professional journey's intimate details. You want your profile to be a beacon for recruiters, a networking hub for fellow professionals, and yet a sanctuary where your privacy is respected. This chapter guides you through setting the proper privacy levels for your activities, connections, and personal information.

The privacy settings on LinkedIn are not just switches to turn on and off; they are strategic tools. They determine who sees your updates, who knows when you make profile changes, and who can view your connections. They're about managing your professional image and taking control of your narrative. For instance, choosing who can see your connections can be a strategic decision - whether you're an open networker looking to grow your contacts widely or a private professional who prefers to keep their network circle close-knit.

Your journey through LinkedIn's privacy settings will also explore how to manage your online visibility. It's about deciding how you appear in search engines and who can view your profile. You'll learn the importance of being discoverable to the right people and how invisibility can sometimes be a hindrance to your career growth.

Then there's the matter of data and ad settings - the backstage of your LinkedIn experience. Navigating these settings is critical to understanding how your data is used and how you can control the ads you see. This chapter will provide insights into managing your data preferences, ensuring your LinkedIn experience aligns with your comfort and expectations.

But what about communication? LinkedIn is not just a profile on a screen; it's a dynamic platform of interactions. Your communication settings determine how you receive messages, who can send you invitations, and how often you're notified about activities. Tailoring these settings is like setting the rhythm of your LinkedIn experience – ensuring you stay connected without being overwhelmed.

In essence, understanding LinkedIn's privacy and settings is akin to mastering the art of digital self-presentation and boundary-setting. This chapter will be your guide in transforming your LinkedIn experience from a default setting to a customized journey, ensuring that your professional identity is both visible and protected.

In the landscape of LinkedIn, your privacy and settings are your compass and map. They guide your journey, protect your course, and ensure that your professional voyage is both safe and rewarding. As we delve deeper into these settings, you will emerge more confident and in control of your LinkedIn presence, ready to harness its full potential while maintaining the sanctity of your professional privacy.

SEE APPENDIX BONUS 1: Detailed Guide to Setting Privacy Parameters on LinkedIn

CHAPTER 2

Crafting a Winning Profile

The Art of a Compelling Headline

Your LinkedIn headline is much more than a mere title; it's your digital handshake, the first impression that announces your professional essence to the world. In the labyrinth of LinkedIn's millions of users, your headline is the beacon that guides the right connections, opportunities, and recruiters to your profile. It's not just a job title; it's a narrative, a promise, a statement of your professional identity.

The headline is your chance to succinctly convey your expertise, your value proposition, and your professional aspirations. It's about crafting a narrative that resonates not only with where you've been but also with where you're aspiring to go. This is particularly crucial for those in mid-career or seeking a career shift. Your headline should bridge the gap between your current position and your career ambitions, capturing the essence of your professional journey and future potential.

Why Your Headline Matters

In the realms of LinkedIn, your headline is your flag – it's what gets seen in searches, connections, and recommendations. It's not just a label; it's a powerful tool that works in the background, enhancing your visibility and relevance in LinkedIn's algorithm. A well-crafted headline makes you discoverable to the right audience – be it a hiring manager in your dream company or a potential business partner.

The Ingredients of a Winning Headline

1. **Clarity and Precision**: Your headline should clearly state what you do or what you specialize in. Avoid jargon or buzzwords that muddy the waters. Be precise and clear.

2. **Showcasing Your Specialty**: Whether you're in IT, finance, or engineering, your headline should reflect your area of expertise. It should answer the question, "What sets me apart in my field?"

3. **Incorporating Keywords**: Think about the terms a recruiter or connection would use to find someone with your skills and expertise. These keywords make your headline search-friendly.

4. **Highlighting Achievements or Aspirations**: If you have a notable achievement or a specific career goal, don't hesitate to weave it into your headline. It shows ambition and direction.

5. **Personal Branding**: Your headline is a prime spot for personal branding. It should echo the unique professional identity you've carved out for yourself.

Crafting Your Headline: A Step-by-Step Approach

1. **Start with Your Job Title**: Begin with the basics – your current role or the primary function of your job. This sets the foundation.

2. **Inject Your Specialization**: Add a phrase that captures your area of expertise or specialization within your field.

3. **Incorporate Keywords**: Weave in keywords that enhance your visibility and align with the roles or opportunities you're targeting.

4. **Flavor with Achievements or Goals**: Include a significant achievement or a clear statement of your professional aspirations.

5. **Polish and Personalize**: Finally, refine your headline for flow and impact. It should feel natural, authentic, and distinctly 'you.'

Examples to Inspire You

- "Senior IT Analyst | Specializing in Cybersecurity Solutions | Aspiring to Lead Enterprise Security Initiatives"

- "Marketing Manager | Brand Development & Digital Strategies | Passionate about Creating Impactful Campaigns"

- "Financial Advisor | Wealth Management Expert | Committed to Innovative Financial Planning for Millennials"

Final Thoughts

Your LinkedIn headline is not set in stone. As your career evolves, so should your headline. It's a dynamic part of your profile, a space that should continually align with your career trajectory. By investing time and thought into crafting a compelling headline, you're not just filling in a section on a profile – you're setting the stage for your next career leap, laying down a path for where you want to go, and inviting the right opportunities to come along.

In this chapter, we've unlocked the secrets to a winning headline. As we delve deeper into crafting your winning LinkedIn profile in the subsequent sections, remember that each part of your profile is a piece of a larger puzzle – your professional story. Let's continue to shape that story with intention, clarity, and foresight.

Experience and Education: Telling Your Story

In the journey of crafting a standout LinkedIn profile, your experience and education are more than just timelines of your professional and academic life. They are the chapters of your unique story; each role and degree is a testament to your growth, skills, and aspirations. In this segment, we delve into how to effectively narrate this story, transforming your experiences and educational background into compelling narratives that resonate with potential employers, recruiters, and connections.

The Narrative of Experience

Your professional experience is the backbone of your LinkedIn profile. It's where you showcase not just where you've worked but how you've made an impact. Each position listed is an opportunity to highlight your accomplishments, skills, and the unique value you brought to the role.

Detailing Roles: Begin by listing your roles, but go beyond the job title. Describe your responsibilities in a way that paints a picture of your day-to-day activities. Use action verbs to give life to your experiences.

Highlighting Achievements: For each role, pinpoint key achievements. Did you increase sales, streamline processes, and lead successful projects? Quantify these successes wherever possible.

Storytelling Your Progression: Show how each role contributed to your growth. A challenge at one job taught you a skill you later used to excel in another. This paints a picture of continuous learning and adaptability.

Bridging Gaps: If there are gaps in your employment, address them honestly. During that time, you pursued further education, freelancing, or personal projects relevant to your career.

Crafting Your Educational Narrative

Your education section is more than a list of degrees; it's an insight into your foundational knowledge and intellectual curiosities. Whether you're a recent graduate or years into your career, your educational background can be a rich source of conversation and connection.

Listing Degrees and Institutions: Start with the basics - your degrees and the institutions where you earned them. Include major fields of study and minors if they are relevant to your career goals.

Extracurricular Involvements: If you were involved in extracurricular activities, especially those related to your career field, mention them. This shows a well-rounded character and initiative.

Continuing Education: If you've taken additional courses or certifications, especially those that have kept your skills current, list them. This shows commitment to continuous personal and professional development.

Academic Achievements: If you have notable academic achievements, such as awards or publications, include them. They demonstrate expertise and dedication.

Integrating Your Story

The art of integrating your experience and education on LinkedIn lies in creating a cohesive narrative. Your profile should not read like a disjointed list of jobs and degrees but as a continuous story of a professional growing, learning, and striving towards specific career goals.

Remember:

Authenticity: Be genuine in how you present your experience and education. Authenticity resonates more than hyperbole.

Relevance: Tailor your profile to reflect the skills and experiences most relevant to where you want your career to go, not just where it has been.

Dynamic Updating: Keep your profile updated as your career progresses. New experiences and education should be added to maintain a current and accurate reflection of your professional journey.

In crafting this section of your profile, you are not just listing your past; you are narrating your professional journey. It's a journey that speaks to your skills, your growth, and, most importantly, the potential you bring to future opportunities. As we go to the following sections, keep in mind that your

LinkedIn profile should change together with you because it is a living record of your professional life.

Skills, Endorsements, and Recommendations

In the world of LinkedIn, your skills, endorsements, and recommendations are the social proof that reinforces your professional narrative. They transform your profile from a self-written resume to a peer-validated resource. This section is where your competencies are not just stated but substantiated, and your professional relationships and reputation come to life.

The Symphony of Skills

Your skills section is a curated list of your professional abilities, but it's more than a mere enumeration. It's about prioritizing skills that are most relevant and current in your field and aligning them with the narrative you've built in your experience and education sections.

Selecting Relevant Skills: Choose skills that are most pertinent to your career goals. If you're in IT, skills like programming languages or software development are essential. In marketing, SEO or social media expertise might be your focus.

Prioritizing Skills: Arrange your skills, starting with the most crucial at the top. LinkedIn allows you to pin your top three skills, ensuring they get the most visibility.

Dynamic Updating: As your career evolves, so should your skills section. Regularly update this section to reflect new abilities and ensure it doesn't become outdated.

Endorsements: The Power of Peer Validation

Endorsements add credibility to your skills. They are quick confirmations from your connections, acknowledging your proficiencies.

Encouraging Endorsements: Feel free to ask colleagues, past employers, or clients to endorse your skills. A polite message reminding them of a project you worked on together can be compelling.

Endorsing Others: Endorsing your connections' skills can often lead to reciprocation. However, always be genuine in your endorsements.

Recommendations: The Personal Testimonials

Recommendations are personal testimonials written by your LinkedIn connections. They are powerful because they come from others who can vouch for your professionalism, work ethic, and skillset.

Seeking Recommendations: Reach out to people you've had significant professional interactions with. It could be a manager, a peer, or a subordinate.

Guiding the Recommendation: When requesting a recommendation, provide a context to the recommender. Mentioning specific projects or achievements can help them write a more focused and impactful recommendation.

Reciprocating the Gesture: If someone writes you a recommendation, consider returning the favor. It not only strengthens your relationship but also enhances your own profile.

Crafting a Story through Social Proof

Imagine your skills, endorsements, and recommendations as a collective story. Each skill you list is a trait of your professional character, each endorsement is an affirmation from your peers, and each recommendation is a chapter narrated by someone who has worked with you. Together, they create a robust image of you as a professional.

Remember:

Authenticity and Integrity: Only list skills you are genuinely proficient in and seek endorsements and recommendations from those who truly know your work.

Quality Over Quantity: It's better to have a few meaningful recommendations than a multitude of generic ones. Similarly, a well-curated list of skills is more impactful than an exhaustive one.

Engagement and Reciprocity: Engage with your network, endorse the skills of others, and show appreciation for recommendations received. This engagement fosters a positive professional community on LinkedIn.

Your skills, endorsements, and recommendations are crucial elements of your LinkedIn profile. They provide a depth and dimension that go beyond the self-reported data. They are endorsements of your professional journey, underlining your expertise and building trust with your network. As you continue to grow in your career, keep these sections reflective of your evolving professional narrative.

Chapter 3

Networking and Building Connections

The Right Way to Connect

In the vast and interconnected world of LinkedIn, building a meaningful network is more art than science. It's about forging connections that are not only numerous but also deep and valuable. The right way to connect on LinkedIn is a blend of strategic thinking, genuine engagement, and a touch of personal flair.

Establishing Your Connection Philosophy

Before you even send out your first invitation, it's crucial to define your connection philosophy. Are you looking to connect broadly with professionals across various industries, or do you prefer a more targeted approach, focusing on people in your field or those who share your interests? This philosophy will guide your networking efforts and help you create a network that aligns with your professional goals and personal values.

Personalizing Connection Requests

When you find someone you'd like to connect with, don't just click the 'Connect' button and hope for the best. Please give it some thought and compose a customized message. Mention how you came across their profile, what you have in common, or why you're interested in connecting with them. This personal touch can be the difference between a declined request and the start of a fruitful professional relationship.

Quality Over Quantity

While it might be tempting to connect with as many people as possible, quality should always trump quantity. It's better to have a smaller network of connections with whom you interact regularly than a vast network of strangers. These quality connections are more likely to lead to meaningful conversations, job opportunities, collaborations, or mentorship.

Engaging With Your Network

Once you've established a connection, don't let it go dormant. Like, remark on, or share your connections' posts to show that you are interested in them. This not only helps in keeping the relationship active but also indicates that you are genuinely interested in their professional lives. Regular engagement can lead to deeper conversations and opportunities that might not surface otherwise.

Offering Value

Networking is a two-way street. Think about what you can offer to your connections. It could be sharing an article, providing insights into your industry, or introducing them to someone in your network. By providing value, you're not just building a network; you're cultivating a community.

Utilizing LinkedIn Groups

Joining groups on LinkedIn that are relevant to your interests or profession can help you grow your network. Participate actively in discussions, share your insights, and connect with other group members. Groups are excellent for finding like-minded professionals and staying updated on industry trends.

Networking Etiquette

Always remember to be respectful and professional in your interactions. If someone doesn't accept your connection request or doesn't reply to your message, it's essential to respect their decision. Networking is as much about building a positive reputation as it is about making connections.

Rekindling Old Connections

Remember to revisit your existing connections. Check-in with former colleagues, classmates, or acquaintances. A simple message asking how they've been or commenting on a recent achievement of theirs can reignite a conversation and bring new opportunities.

Networking with a Purpose

Every connection you make should have a purpose. Whether it's learning from their experience, collaborating on a project, or expanding your reach in a new industry, having a clear intention behind your connections will make your networking efforts more focused and fruitful.

Reflecting and Refining

Regularly take stock of your network. Assess if your connections align with your career goals and whether they add value to your professional life. Don't hesitate to refine your network if needed. This might mean connecting with new people or even disconnecting from those who don't align with your professional path.

Networking on LinkedIn is an ongoing process of building, engaging, and nurturing professional relationships. It's about connecting with purpose, engaging with authenticity, and continuously refining your network to align with your evolving career goals. Remember, the right connections can open doors to opportunities and experiences beyond your imagination.

Networking Strategies for Success

Networking on LinkedIn transcends beyond expanding your professional circle; it's an art of cultivating meaningful relationships that foster mutual growth and opportunities. The key to successful networking lies in a proactive approach, where you don't just wait for opportunities to knock but actively seek and create them. Begin by researching and identifying key individuals in your industry and understanding their interests and career paths. This guides you in making your interactions more relevant and meaningful.

Engagement is the lifeblood of effective networking. Participate actively by commenting on posts, sharing insightful articles, and joining discussions. This not only elevates your visibility but also cements your position as a contributing member of your professional community. Remember, effective networking is a balance of give and take.

Utilize LinkedIn's features strategically. Engage with alumni, follow companies, participate in LinkedIn Groups, and attend virtual events and webinars. These platforms provide a plethora of opportunities to learn, engage, and connect with professionals who share your interests. In these settings, being an active participant is crucial – engaging in discussions, asking questions, and following up with connections post-event.

Cultivating relationships is a gradual process that requires regular interaction, sharing of relevant information, and support for each other's achievements. Diversify your network by connecting with professionals from various industries and backgrounds, as this broadens your perspective and opens doors to unforeseen opportunities. Your personal brand on LinkedIn significantly influences your networking success. Make sure that your profile appropriately conveys your experience and the unique value that you offer.

Follow-ups are integral to solidifying new connections. After making a new connection or having a discussion, send a personalized thank you message or a summary note. This meticulousness establishes a formal tone for your interactions. Recommendations are another powerful tool on LinkedIn. Seek and offer testimonials to enhance credibility and professional reputation.

While LinkedIn offers a robust platform for online networking, complement this with offline interactions. Attend industry events, join local groups, and participate in community gatherings to strengthen your network. Regularly reflect on your networking strategy and its alignment with your career goals. Be adaptable and ready to refine your approach for maximum efficacy.

In conclusion, successful networking on LinkedIn is about strategy, authenticity, and continuous engagement. It involves building a network that not only supports your career aspirations but also offers you opportunities to contribute meaningfully. With these strategies, your LinkedIn network can become a dynamic and supportive community, opening doors to a wealth of professional opportunities and experiences.

Engaging with Your Network

Engaging with your network on LinkedIn is akin to nurturing a garden; it requires consistent care, attention, and a personalized touch. Engagement is not just about expanding your network; it's about cultivating deep, meaningful connections that can lead to fruitful collaborations and opportunities.

First and foremost, understand the interests and needs of your network. This involves staying active and informed about their updates, achievements, and discussions. When you interact with their content through likes, comments, or shares, ensure your engagement is thoughtful and adds value. Generic comments will not make you stand out, but personalized, insightful inputs can significantly impact your connections and show that you genuinely care about their content.

Content sharing is a powerful tool for engagement. Share articles, insights, or experiences that resonate with your professional journey and are likely to interest your connections. This not only showcases your expertise but also invites dialogue and interaction. However, remember that quality trumps quantity. It's better to share fewer, high-quality posts that genuinely engage your audience than to bombard them with content.

Regular interaction is vital. Don't just reach out to your connections when you need a favor. Make regular, non-intrusive contact by congratulating them on milestones or commenting on their posts. This helps in keeping the connection warm and genuine.

Hosting or participating in LinkedIn Live sessions or webinars can also be an excellent way to engage with your network. Through these platforms, you can impart your knowledge, interact with your connections in real-time, and learn new skills from others.

Mentoring or seeking mentorship is another significant aspect of engagement. Sharing your knowledge and expertise with someone just starting in your field or seeking advice from more experienced professionals can be incredibly rewarding and enriching for both parties.

Remember to engage outside your immediate network. Commenting on and sharing content from industry influencers or thought leaders can not only provide you with valuable insights but also expose you to a broader audience.

Chapter 4

Leveraging LinkedIn for Job Hunting

The Hidden Job Market on LinkedIn

The hidden job market on LinkedIn is a dynamic and often underutilized realm, brimming with opportunities that never make it to public job boards. This market provides a wealth of options for the astute job seeker, provided they have the appropriate tactics and insights.

In this hidden market, opportunities are often filled through connections, internal referrals, and proactive candidate searches by recruiters. It's a domain where your network's strength, your professional brand, and how effectively you engage on LinkedIn significantly influence your job prospects.

To tap into this hidden market, start by building a robust network of connections. Connect with professionals in your industry, including peers, mentors, and industry leaders. The broader and more engaged your network, the higher your chances of learning about unadvertised opportunities. It's not just about the number of connections but the quality of relationships and interactions within your network that counts.

Be an active participant on LinkedIn. Regularly update your profile, share relevant content, and engage in discussions. This visibility increases your chances of being noticed by recruiters and hiring managers who very often use LinkedIn to search for potential candidates. By sharing insights, commenting on industry news, and contributing to conversations, you position yourself as a knowledgeable and active industry player.

Utilize LinkedIn's advanced search capabilities to find and follow companies of interest. Many companies have a LinkedIn presence where they may share updates on company culture, achievements, and, occasionally, unadvertised job openings. By following these companies, you get insights into their needs and can tailor your profile and interactions to catch their attention.

Seek out and join LinkedIn Groups related to your field. These groups are often a goldmine for insider information, networking opportunities, and unadvertised job openings. Participate in discussions, offer value, and establish yourself as an engaged and knowledgeable professional.

Leverage the power of informational interviews. Reach out to professionals in companies where you'd like to work and ask for informational interviews. These conversations may lead to unannounced career opportunities as well as insightful information about the organization.

Remember, your approach should be tailored and strategic. When reaching out to new connections, personalize your requests. Explain why you're interested in connecting and how you might provide value to them rather than making it solely about your job search.

The hidden job market on LinkedIn is a landscape of potential, and the key to unlocking its opportunities lies in proactive networking, strategic engagement, and personal brand building. By cultivating a strong professional presence on LinkedIn, you position yourself to tap into this rich market, where opportunities are often found through connections, engagement, and visibility.

Finally, remember that engagement is a two-way street. Be responsive to those who reach out to you, whether it's a question, a comment on your post, or a request for advice. Acknowledging and appreciating their effort in reaching out goes a long way in building solid and lasting relationships.

In conclusion, engaging with your network on LinkedIn requires a strategic, thoughtful approach. It's about building a community, sharing knowledge, and creating a supportive professional ecosystem. By actively engaging with your network, you open doors to new opportunities, insights, and deeper professional relationships.

Advanced Search Techniques

Mastering the advanced search techniques on LinkedIn is akin to unlocking a treasure trove of job opportunities. This powerful tool, when utilized efficiently, can refine your job hunt, leading you to opportunities that align precisely with your career aspirations and skill set. In this digital age, where a vast number of job seekers are vying for attention on LinkedIn, standing out requires not just a compelling profile but also a savvy approach to finding and applying for jobs.

The first step in leveraging LinkedIn's advanced search is to familiarize yourself with its filters. You can use these filters to focus just on the most pertinent chances when searching. It is possible to filter jobs based on experience level, company size, industry, and location. This focused strategy guarantees that you won't waste time on listings that don't meet your requirements.

Keywords are your best ally in this endeavor. Use specific, industry-related keywords in your searches to find the most relevant job postings. For instance, if you are a software engineer specializing in artificial intelligence, your keywords might include "AI engineer," "machine learning," and "software development." The more specific your keywords, the more tailored your job search results will be.

Another significant aspect of advanced job searching on LinkedIn involves setting up job alerts. Once you have a clear idea of the type of roles you are interested in, set up alerts with these criteria. LinkedIn will notify you via email or through the platform whenever a job that matches your specified criteria is posted. This proactive approach means you can be one of the first applicants, giving you a competitive edge.

To fully utilize the possibilities of modern search techniques, networking is essential. When you find a job that interests you, check if you have any connections at the hiring company. A referral from a current employee can significantly increase your chances of landing an interview.

Even if you do not have a direct connection, you may find a second or third-degree connection willing to make an introduction.

Utilize the 'People Also Viewed' feature on LinkedIn. When you visit a company's LinkedIn page, this feature shows you profiles of people who have viewed that company. This can lead to discovering potential hiring managers or recruiters. Connecting with these professionals, accompanied by a well-crafted message, can open doors to opportunities that are not advertised publicly.

Keep in mind that using LinkedIn for a job hunt is about more than just applying to jobs that are posted. It involves a blend of targeted searches, timely applications, and strategic networking. By mastering these advanced search techniques, you position yourself not just as a candidate who applies for jobs but as a proactive professional who strategically navigates and harnesses the full potential of LinkedIn in the job market.

In essence, LinkedIn's advanced search is not merely a feature; it's a pathway to your next career opportunity. By understanding and utilizing these advanced techniques, you are not just searching for a job; you are strategically positioning yourself for the career growth you envision.

Inizio modulo

SEE APPENDIX BONUS 2: Detailed Guide to Setting Privacy Parameters on LinkedIn

Applying for Jobs via LinkedIn

Applying for jobs via LinkedIn is a journey that blends strategy with personal branding. As a digital era job seeker, you must recognize the power of LinkedIn, not just as a networking platform but as a critical tool in your job application arsenal. This chapter takes you through an integrated approach to applying for jobs on LinkedIn, offering a blend of practical steps, insights, and strategies to elevate your job application process.

The journey begins with understanding the LinkedIn application process, which has been designed to simplify job applications by integrating them within the platform. It offers a streamlined experience, allowing you to apply for positions directly through LinkedIn, often with just a few clicks. But caution is key; each application for a job should be customized for the particular position and employer. This means customizing your resume, crafting a personalized cover letter, and ensuring your LinkedIn profile echoes the skills and experiences most relevant to the job.

The 'Easy Apply' feature on LinkedIn is a fantastic tool, but it's essential to know when to use it effectively. While it offers convenience, sometimes a more personalized application directly through the company's website may be more advantageous. Alongside this, leverage the wealth of company information available on LinkedIn to understand their culture and values, enabling you to tailor your application to resonate more profoundly with the employer.

Once you've applied, the process doesn't end there. Following up is a critical step. Knowing how to send a thoughtful message to the recruiter or hiring manager via LinkedIn can keep you engaged with the company and demonstrate your genuine interest in the role. In parallel, setting up job alerts on LinkedIn ensures you're constantly in the loop with new opportunities that match your career interests.

Handling application rejections with grace and using them as learning experiences is also a vital skill. LinkedIn can be used to maintain a positive professional relationship with companies, keeping the door open for future opportunities. Additionally, continuously updating and optimizing your LinkedIn profile, even while applying for jobs, reflects your evolving skills and career objectives.

Understanding job application trends on LinkedIn, such as roles in high demand and sought-after skills, can help align your career trajectory with market demands, making your applications timelier and more relevant. Finally, building a supportive network on LinkedIn can provide not only moral support but also practical advice, recommendations, and insider information about job openings and company cultures.

This chapter aims to transform your view of LinkedIn from a mere social platform to a powerful ally in your job search journey. By the end of it, you'll be equipped with the knowledge and tools to use LinkedIn effectively, proactively, and successfully in your pursuit of career growth and fulfillment.

Chapter 5

Personal Branding and Content Creation

Establishing Your Personal Brand

In the digital era, establishing a personal brand on LinkedIn transcends mere resume display. It's an art form, a strategic endeavor to distinguish oneself in a vast professional network. Your unique value proposition, the professional DNA, should define your LinkedIn presence. It's not just about listing skills or experiences; it's about crafting a narrative that resonates with your audience, whether potential employers, clients, or collaborators.

Think of your LinkedIn headline as your virtual handshake, your introduction to the professional world. It should encapsulate more than just your current job title; it should echo your professional story, your ambitions, and your unique perspective. The summary section is where this story gains depth and personality. Here, your professional journey should unfold, highlighting not only what you've achieved but also how these experiences have shaped your professional identity.

Visual elements like a professional profile photo and a background image that reflects your professional persona can significantly amplify your brand. Consistency in these visuals across various platforms can strengthen your brand's impact. The experience section should be more than a list of job titles; it should showcase the impact and contributions you've made in your career. Utilize metrics and specific achievements that align with your brand and showcase your expertise.

On LinkedIn, content production is an effective strategy for developing thought leadership. Sharing insights, writing articles, and engaging with content relevant to your field can reinforce your brand and establish you as a thought leader. Engaging authentically with your network through comments, discussions, and group participation is crucial. This engagement should reflect your brand and contribute meaningfully to conversations in your field.

Endorsements and recommendations provide social proof of your brand, adding credibility to your narrative. They should reflect the essential skills and strengths central to your personal brand. Remember, your personal brand is dynamic, evolving with your career. Regularly update your profile, engage with emerging trends in your field, and adapt your strategy to reflect your growth and learning.

Consistency in presentation, communication, and engagement is key to solidifying your personal brand on LinkedIn. Every interaction and content piece should align with the professional identity you've cultivated. By doing so, you create a cohesive and compelling image that not only stands out in the digital realm but also opens up new avenues for professional opportunities and growth. Your LinkedIn profile, thus, becomes more than just a platform for networking; it's a canvas for your personal brand, a testament to your unique professional journey.

Creating and Sharing Content

Crafting and sharing engaging content on LinkedIn is an integral part of personal branding, especially for professionals aiming to elevate their career trajectory. It's not just about posting regularly; it's about crafting a story that appeals to your intended audience, be it mid-career professionals in IT, finance, or engineering or dynamic women breaking the glass ceiling in their respective fields.

Start by understanding your audience's needs and interests. This could range from career development tips to the latest in technology or financial planning. Your content should not only showcase your expertise but also provide tangible value. Whether it's through insightful articles, quick posts, or engaging videos, ensure that your content is diverse and caters to various preferences within your audience.

Storytelling is a powerful tool. Share your journey, the lessons you've learned, and your professional experiences. This approach not only humanizes your profile but also makes your content relatable and compelling. Engaging with trending topics in your industry shows that you are current and active in relevant conversations. Pose queries and start conversations to elicit responses from readers on your posts. This engagement goes beyond your content - regularly interact with others' posts to build a genuine presence on the platform.

Consistency in posting is key. A regular schedule keeps you relevant and helps in building a loyal audience base. However, it's crucial to analyze the engagement on your posts. Recognize what appeals to your audience and modify your approach accordingly. Professional presentation is non-negotiable – maintain a tone and style that reflects your professional image, including proper grammar and appropriate visuals.

Lastly, don't shy away from sharing success stories and testimonials. These add credibility and showcase the practical application of your skills and expertise. In summary, your LinkedIn content strategy should be a thoughtful blend of expertise sharing, storytelling, and audience engagement, all wrapped in a consistent, professional package. Remember, every piece of content contributes to building your personal brand and should align with your career goals and the interests of your target audience.

Thought Leadership on LinkedIn

Establishing yourself as a thought leader on LinkedIn requires a blend of expertise, authenticity, and strategic content creation. Here's a comprehensive approach to achieving this:

Start by identifying your niche, focusing on areas where your expertise and passion intersect. Whether it's technology, finance, engineering, or any other field, your unique perspective is your greatest asset. This niche should be the cornerstone of your content strategy on LinkedIn.

Content is paramount in thought leadership. Share insights, articles, infographics, or videos that not only showcase your knowledge but also provide value to your audience. Address current trends, offer solutions to common industry problems, or present new perspectives. Quality should always be prioritized over quantity – a well-researched, insightful post once a week can be more impactful than daily posts with less substance.

Active engagement is crucial. Participate in conversations, answer comments on your posts, and interact with your readers. This not only increases your visibility but also helps you gain a deeper understanding of your audience's needs and preferences.

Make the most of LinkedIn's features. Publish articles on LinkedIn Pulse or host discussions and webinars using LinkedIn Live. These tools can significantly boost your reach and engagement levels.

Collaborate with other thought leaders and influencers. This can expand your reach and bring diverse perspectives to your content. Networking and collaborating on LinkedIn can open doors to new audiences and enrich your content.

Consistency in posting is key but be prepared to evolve your approach based on feedback and changing trends. Examine your LinkedIn analytics on a regular basis to find out what kinds of material are most popular with your audience.

Sharing personal stories and experiences adds a relatable and human element to your content. Narratives about overcoming challenges or unique career experiences can be particularly engaging and inspiring.

Showcase your commitment to professional growth. Share insights from conferences or workshops you've attended, or talk about how recent courses have influenced your professional perspective.

Be receptive to feedback. Constructive criticism can guide your content strategy and help you refine your approach to meet the needs of your audience better.

Above all, maintain authenticity and integrity. Your content should be a true reflection of your professional identity and values. Authenticity is what differentiates a genuine thought leader from a mere content creator.

In summary, becoming a thought leader on LinkedIn is about finding your unique voice, consistently creating and sharing valuable content, engaging with your audience, and staying true to your professional ethos. This journey requires patience, commitment, and a genuine desire to contribute to your industry.

Chapter 6

LinkedIn and Recruiters

Understanding the Recruiter's Perspective

In the interconnected world of LinkedIn, understanding the recruiter's perspective is crucial for anyone aiming to advance their career. Recruiters use LinkedIn as a tool to not only find candidates with the right skills and experience but also to identify individuals who fit well within their company culture.

There is more to your LinkedIn page than just an online CV; it's a platform for you to tell your professional story. A compelling profile doesn't just list your experiences and skills but also paints a picture of your career journey, achievements, and potential. It should reflect not only your professional abilities but also give insights into your personality and work ethic. This narrative is what makes you stand out to recruiters looking for a candidate that aligns with their company's values and culture.

Recruiters often target not just active job seekers but also passive candidates - those not actively looking for a new job but open to exciting opportunities. Keeping your profile updated with your latest achievements and career developments makes you visible and appealing to this group of recruiters.

Keywords play a significant role in how recruiters find potential candidates. Including relevant industry and role-specific keywords in your profile boosts your visibility in search results, drawing recruiter attention your way. Understanding and applying LinkedIn SEO principles can significantly enhance your profile's discoverability.

Engagement on LinkedIn also counts. Regular contributions to discussions, posting insightful content, and being active in relevant groups demonstrate your commitment and expertise in your field. Such engagement can position you as a thought leader and make your profile more attractive to recruiters.

Recommendations and endorsements give your profile more legitimacy. These testimonials from colleagues, managers, and other professional contacts act as a stamp of approval for your skills and work history, making your profile more trustworthy in the eyes of recruiters.

Beyond professional qualifications, recruiters on LinkedIn are also looking for candidates who would be an excellent cultural fit for their organization. Your interactions, the content you share, and the overall tone of your profile can offer insights into your personality and work style. Being authentic and showcasing your personal brand can attract recruiters looking for someone who will mesh well with their team.

Understanding LinkedIn's privacy settings is also necessary. While visibility to recruiters is key, managing what information you make public is crucial for maintaining your online professionalism and privacy.

Lastly, your communication with recruiters should always be professional, whether you're interested in the opportunity or not. Building and maintaining a network of recruiter connections can lead to more opportunities in the future. Engaging politely and professionally with recruiters, regardless of your interest in the role, helps in expanding your professional network on LinkedIn.

In summary, grasping the recruiter's perspective on LinkedIn involves more than just showcasing your professional skills. It requires a holistic approach: crafting a narrative-driven profile, optimizing it with the right keywords, actively engaging with your network, demonstrating your personality, and maintaining professional interactions. You may significantly increase your chances of being recognized and appreciated by recruiters in your field by doing this.

Making Yourself Visible to Recruiters

Enhancing Visibility to Recruiters on LinkedIn making yourself visible to recruiters on LinkedIn involves a blend of profile optimization, active engagement, and strategic networking. Begin by ensuring your profile is comprehensive and up-to-date, reflecting your professional journey with clarity and precision. Incorporate a professional photo and craft a compelling headline that extends beyond your current job title. Your summary should narrate your career story, underlining your unique value proposition.

Incorporate relevant keywords throughout your profile. These are the terms that recruiters commonly use to search for candidates in your field. Embedding these keywords in your headline, summary, and job descriptions boosts your chances of appearing in search results.

Activate LinkedIn's 'Open to Work' feature, which discreetly informs recruiters that you're seeking new opportunities. Specify the job roles, industries, and locations you're interested in to guide recruiters to your profile.

Regular content sharing and publishing on LinkedIn is crucial. Engage with your network through thoughtful articles, industry insights, and participation in relevant discussions. This not only increases your visibility but also establishes you as a knowledgeable professional in your field.

Networking plays a crucial role. Expand your connections to include colleagues, industry peers, and other professionals. A broader network means greater visibility. Engage actively by commenting on posts, joining discussions, and being part of LinkedIn groups related to your industry.

Showcase your professional achievements and skills. Share projects, publications, or awards to highlight your capabilities. Recommendations from colleagues or managers add credibility to your profile and serve as endorsements for your skills and work ethic.

Pay attention to LinkedIn analytics. Monitoring who views your profile can offer insights into the types of recruiters and organizations showing interest in your background. This information can help you tailor your profile and content strategy.

Maintain a high level of professionalism in your profile's presentation. Regular updates to reflect new skills or experiences keep your profile current and relevant.

In summary, making yourself visible to recruiters on LinkedIn is about

strategically shaping your profile, staying active and engaged in your

professional network, and using LinkedIn's features effectively. It's a dynamic process of presenting your professional narrative, showcasing your achievements, and building a network that aligns with your career aspirations. With these approaches, you enhance your chances of catching the eye of recruiters and opening doors to new career opportunities.

SEE APPENDIX BONUS 3: Creating a Comprehensive LinkedIn Profile that Reflects Your Professional Journey

Interacting with Recruiters

In the contemporary job market, LinkedIn stands as a pivotal platform connecting job seekers with recruiters. The art of engaging with recruiters on this platform requires a nuanced understanding of both the digital medium and the human element of professional networking. With the help of this tutorial, you can communicate with recruiters on LinkedIn more effectively and enjoy a more successful job hunt.

Creating a Recruiter-Attractive Profile: Your LinkedIn profile is the gateway to professional opportunities. Craft it meticulously to ensure it resonates with recruiters.

Incorporate industry-relevant keywords, and don't shy away from showcasing your accomplishments. A professional photo adds a touch of personality.

Initiating Contact Thoughtfully: When reaching out to recruiters, personalization is critical. Tailor your connection requests by referencing specific aspects of the recruiter's profile or job postings. Clearly state your intentions, be it active job searching or general networking.

Effective Communication Post-Connection: Once connected, balance professionalism with brevity in your communications. Engage in meaningful conversations by asking insightful questions. Show genuine

interest in the industry and the recruiter's expertise. Remember, following up is good, but pestering is not.

Empathizing with Recruiters: Understanding a recruiter's role and challenges can significantly improve your communication. They often juggle multiple roles and candidates, so patience is crucial. Be prompt in providing any requested information and articulate your career goals

clearly to facilitate easier job matching.

Fostering Long-term Relationships: Building a lasting relationship with recruiters can open doors to future opportunities. Stay in touch, even after securing a job. Offering referrals and engaging with their content keeps the relationship dynamic and reciprocal. A simple thank you

can go a long way in nurturing this professional bond.

Summing Up: The crux of successful interactions with recruiters on LinkedIn lies in understanding the platform's nuances and maintaining professionalism. By crafting an appealing profile, initiating personalized contact, engaging thoughtfully, understanding the recruiter's perspective, and nurturing ongoing relationships, you can effectively harness LinkedIn's potential in your career progression. This approach not only aids in the immediate job search but also lays the groundwork for sustained professional growth and networking.

Chapter 7

Preparing for Interviews and Negotiations

LinkedIn Insights for Interview Preparation

In the landscape of modern job hunting, LinkedIn stands out as a multifaceted tool crucial for interview preparation. This platform, teeming with professional insights and resources, can be strategically used to give job seekers an edge in the competitive market. This chapter explores various ways to utilize LinkedIn for adequate interview preparation.

Firstly, LinkedIn serves as an excellent resource for in-depth company research. By following the company's LinkedIn page, you gain access to their updates, achievements, and cultural insights. This knowledge not only prepares you for specific company-related questions but also demonstrates your genuine interest and diligence.

Understanding your interviewer's background can also be pivotal. LinkedIn profiles of your interviewers can provide valuable context about their professional journey, interests, and expertise. Knowing these details can help tailor your approach and build rapport during the interview.

Keeping abreast of industry trends is another critical aspect of interview preparation. LinkedIn is a hub for following industry leaders, engaging in relevant groups, and participating in discussions. This continual engagement showcases your commitment to the industry and keeps you informed about current trends and topics.

Enhancing relevant skills is another benefit of LinkedIn. Through LinkedIn Learning, you can access a plethora of courses and resources that align with the job role you're interviewing for. Whether it's a technical skill or industry knowledge, sharpening your abilities can give you a notable advantage.

Networking plays a significant role in preparation, too. Utilizing your LinkedIn connections for mock interviews can provide constructive feedback and boost confidence. These interactions also deepen your professional relationships.

Your LinkedIn profile itself is a powerful tool for conveying your professional brand. Ensuring your profile accurately reflects your professional narrative, skills, and aspirations is crucial. A compelling summary, professional photograph, and detailed experience sections can significantly influence the interviewer's perception of you.

Preparing thoughtful questions based on your LinkedIn research can further demonstrate your proactive approach. Inquiring about the company's recent developments or industry shifts indicates your thorough preparation and enthusiasm.

Finally, post-interview, LinkedIn can be a reflective space. Sharing your experiences and insights or seeking advice from your network fosters a culture of continuous learning and community support.

In summary, LinkedIn's diverse features, from company research and skill enhancement to networking and personal branding, provide a comprehensive approach to interview preparation. Harnessing these facets can not only prepare you for the interview but also position you as a well-informed, engaged, and proactive candidate.

Salary Insights and Job Market Trends

Leveraging LinkedIn for Salary Insights and Job Market Trends

Navigating the modern job market requires a keen understanding of salary standards and industry trends. LinkedIn, as a comprehensive professional platform, offers unique tools and insights that empower individuals to stay informed and competitive. Here's a cohesive exploration of how LinkedIn can be a game-changer in understanding salary insights and job market trends:

Unveiling Salary Insights

LinkedIn's salary tool is a goldmine for gaining a realistic view of potential earnings. By entering specific job titles, industries, and locations, users can access a detailed salary range, inclusive of base pay, bonuses, and additional compensation. This data, sourced from a vast pool of user-contributed information, is pivotal for setting realistic salary expectations. The tool's confidentiality assurance encourages honest data input, enhancing its reliability. Additionally, the comparison feature and various filters like experience, education, and company size allow for a more nuanced and personalized salary analysis.

Deciphering Job Market Trends

Beyond just job listings, LinkedIn serves as a pulse check on the job market. It curates relevant industry news and articles, offering insights into emerging trends and technological shifts. Following industry influencers and thought leaders exposes users to expert opinions and predictions, while regular analysis of job postings reveals changes in demanded skills and industry priorities. LinkedIn Learning aligns with these trends, offering courses in high-demand skills. Moreover, engaging with your network and participating in discussions provides firsthand insights into industry movements. The platform's advanced search filters also aid in identifying patterns and shifts in job openings and requirements.

Strategic Career Planning

Integrating salary insights with job market trends empowers professionals to make informed decisions. This knowledge is crucial for effective job negotiations and strategic career planning. Understanding the value of your skills in the market, what employers are willing to pay, and the direction your industry is heading equips you with the confidence to make career moves that align with both your personal goals and market dynamics.

In essence, LinkedIn transcends its role as a networking site to become a valuable resource for salary and market trend insights. By leveraging these tools, professionals can negotiate confidently, plan strategically, and remain at the forefront of their industry's evolution. This approach ensures they are not only well-informed but also well-prepared to navigate the complexities of the modern job market.

SEE APPENDIX BONUS 4: LinkedIn Salary Tool: Your Guide to Understanding Potential Earnings

Negotiation Strategies

In the realm of professional advancement, negotiating effectively is crucial. It's a skill that's essential not only for salary discussions but also for various aspects of job offers and career growth. This chapter delves into pivotal negotiation strategies, with a focus on leveraging LinkedIn's resources for optimal outcomes.

Firstly, understanding your worth in the job market is paramount. LinkedIn provides a wealth of data to assess average salaries, benefits, and industry standards, allowing you to establish a baseline for negotiations. Next, it's crucial to build a strong case for your value. This involves highlighting your skills, experiences, and achievements, backed by endorsements and recommendations visible on your LinkedIn profile.

Instead of viewing negotiations as a confrontation, they should be viewed as a cooperative endeavor. Open, honest discussions about career goals, aligned with the company's objectives, create a constructive environment for negotiations. Additionally, using LinkedIn to understand a company's culture and values can be instrumental in tailoring your negotiation strategy to fit their ethos.

Flexibility and a willingness to compromise are also crucial in negotiations. Monetary compensation isn't the only valuable aspect; consider non-monetary benefits that may align better with your career and life goals. LinkedIn can also be a source of creative compensation strategies prevalent in your industry.

Being prepared for various negotiation scenarios is another vital strategy. Connecting with mentors and industry experts on LinkedIn, practicing your negotiation skills, and preparing for potential counterarguments can significantly enhance your confidence and effectiveness in negotiations.

Lastly, viewing negotiation as an ongoing learning process is vital for long-term career success. LinkedIn serves as a continuous learning platform, offering insights from industry thought leaders and keeping you updated on new trends and strategies in negotiation.

In essence, effective negotiation involves a deep understanding of your market value, clear communication of your capabilities, a collaborative mindset, flexibility in terms and conditions, thorough preparation for various scenarios, and a commitment to continuous learning and growth. Utilizing LinkedIn as a resource in this process can significantly influence your negotiation success and, consequently, your career progression.

Chapter 8

Staying Ahead: Continuous Learning and Growth

Utilizing LinkedIn Learning

This section is dedicated to "Utilizing LinkedIn Learning" and its significance in the journey of continuous growth.

LinkedIn Learning, an expansive online educational platform, offers a wide array of courses spanning various fields, including business, technology, and creative topics. Its integration with LinkedIn's professional network provides a unique advantage – the ability to tailor learning experiences based on industry trends, job roles, and skills required in the market.

LinkedIn Learning is an invaluable resource for people looking to grow in their careers. The platform's algorithm suggests courses based on your current skills, job title, and what other professionals in similar roles are learning. This personalized approach ensures that you're not just learning randomly but strategically enhancing skills that bolster your professional profile.

The courses on LinkedIn Learning are designed to be practical and applicable in real-world scenarios. They range from short tutorials to comprehensive learning paths, allowing for flexibility in learning pace and style. For example, an IT professional might find courses on the latest programming languages, while a marketing manager might explore classes on digital marketing trends.

Beyond individual course offerings, LinkedIn Learning provides an opportunity to demonstrate your commitment to self-improvement. By completing courses and adding these skills to your LinkedIn profile, you not only keep your profile updated but also showcase your proactive approach to potential employers or collaborators.

Moreover, LinkedIn Learning is a powerful tool for staying abreast of evolving industry standards and practices. With courses developed by industry experts, it provides insights into emerging trends, ensuring that your skillset remains relevant in a rapidly changing job market.

For mid-career professionals, LinkedIn Learning offers a path to pivot or advance within their current industry. For instance, an engineer might pursue project management courses to move into a management role or a finance professional might explore fintech courses to transition into a burgeoning field.

In summary, LinkedIn Learning is more than just an educational resource; it's a strategic tool for career advancement and personal growth. It enables professionals to stay ahead in their fields, adapt to new challenges, and seize opportunities in an ever-evolving job market. This chapter not only guides you through maximizing the benefits of LinkedIn Learning but also emphasizes its role in a strategy for lifelong learning and career progression.

SEE APPENDIX BONUS 5: Understanding LinkedIn Learning

Growing Your Career Post Job-Search

After getting hired, developing your career is a path that calls for constant work and thoughtful preparation. LinkedIn offers a wealth of resources to support this continuous growth. Here's a detailed guide on leveraging LinkedIn for sustained career development:

Firstly, LinkedIn isn't just for job searching; it's a hub for career advancement. Engage actively with learning opportunities, industry groups, and discussions relevant to your field. Share insights, participate in conversations, and stay abreast of the latest trends. This active involvement keeps you informed and engaged in your professional community.

Networking is key to long-term career success. Forge connections with colleagues, industry leaders, and mentors on LinkedIn. Engage with your network by sharing content, commenting on posts, and joining groups. These relationships may present advantageous new prospects as well as essential industry insights.

Your LinkedIn profile should reflect your growing expertise. Regularly update it with your latest achievements, skills, and projects. Articulate your successes in a way that showcases your contributions and learning experiences.

Personal branding is crucial in today's job market. Use LinkedIn to develop a brand aligned with your career aspirations. Share articles, blog posts, and your insights to position yourself as a thought leader in your field. This enhances your visibility and reputation in your industry.

Immerse yourself in your company's culture and LinkedIn initiatives. Participate in company discussions and groups. Understanding the company dynamics and aligning your goals with the organization's objectives can be incredibly beneficial.

Feedback is a valuable tool for growth. Use LinkedIn to seek constructive feedback from peers and mentors. Discussions about performance and improvement areas can offer essential insights for your professional development.

Setting clear, achievable career goals is vital. Use LinkedIn to research successful professionals' paths and understand the skills and experiences behind their success. Regularly revisit and adjust your goals to align with your career progression and industry developments.

Commit to lifelong learning. Engage in LinkedIn Learning courses relevant to your field to stay current and adaptable. This demonstrates your dedication to professional growth.

Lastly, build a supportive community on LinkedIn. Share your knowledge and job opportunities, and endorse others' skills. A supportive network creates a positive professional environment that's beneficial for everyone involved.

In conclusion, leveraging LinkedIn effectively means engaging with the platform far beyond the job search phase. It's about creating a dynamic and interactive professional presence, continuously learning, networking strategically, and contributing to the community. By doing so, you not only enhance your own career but also contribute positively to your broader professional network.

Future-Proofing Your Career on LinkedIn

Future-proofing your career in today's fast-paced job market requires a strategic approach, and LinkedIn is an invaluable tool in this endeavor. It's not just about keeping your profile updated or networking; it's about a holistic strategy that aligns with the dynamic nature of industries and job roles. Here's how you can use LinkedIn to ensure your career remains resilient and future-proof:

Proactive Profile Updates: Regularly refreshing your LinkedIn profile is more than just adding new job titles. It's about showcasing your growth and adaptability. Highlight your evolving skills, projects, and learning experiences that demonstrate your ability to stay ahead in your field.

Leveraging LinkedIn Learning: Embrace continuous learning by diving into LinkedIn Learning courses. These tools help you stay up to date with the newest trends and technologies by spanning a variety of industries and skill sets. Displaying these learning endeavors on your profile signals to potential employers your dedication to growth.

Diverse Networking: Cultivate a diverse network beyond your immediate field. Engage with professionals across different areas, participate in discussions, and attend LinkedIn's virtual events and webinars. Such a network can open doors to unexpected opportunities and insights.

Engaging with Industry Insights: Follow industry leaders, companies, and influencers on LinkedIn for valuable insights. Enroll in groups tailored to your sector to participate in conversations and gain knowledge from colleagues' combined experiences.

Establishing Thought Leadership: Share insightful content, comment thoughtfully on industry news, and engage with others' posts to position yourself as a thought leader. This not only enhances your visibility but also establishes your expertise.

Adapting to Industry Shifts: Keep an eye on the changing trends in your industry. LinkedIn's job market trends and salary insights are valuable for understanding market dynamics and helping you anticipate changes and adapt accordingly.

Feedback and Mentorship: Actively seek feedback and mentorship through LinkedIn. Connecting with mentors and peers for guidance can help you identify improvement areas and new growth directions.

Aligning Goals with Market Trends: Regularly evaluate and realign your career goals with the market needs. This means assessing your career path and making adjustments based on growth areas and opportunities reflected in the LinkedIn landscape.

In essence, future-proofing your career with LinkedIn involves a continuous cycle of learning, adapting, and networking. It's about positioning yourself as a flexible, informed, and proactive professional who is ready to embrace the changes and opportunities the future holds.

Conclusion

In wrapping up this comprehensive guide on leveraging LinkedIn for career advancement, it's crucial to underscore the overarching theme: LinkedIn is more than a job-hunting platform; it's a dynamic tool for continual professional development and networking. The chapters of this book have systematically laid out strategies for optimizing every aspect of LinkedIn, from creating a standout profile and effectively networking to interacting with recruiters and preparing for interviews.

Remember, your LinkedIn journey doesn't end with securing a job. It's about ongoing growth and adaptation in a rapidly evolving professional landscape. Regularly updating your profile, actively engaging with your network, and utilizing resources like LinkedIn Learning are essential steps to keep your career trajectory upward and forward-moving.

The power of LinkedIn lies not just in its ability to connect you with job opportunities but in its role as a gateway to a global professional community. This platform is an invaluable resource for gaining industry insights, sharing knowledge, and accessing mentorship and collaborative opportunities. By actively participating in this community, you open doors to unexpected prospects and career advancements.

As you step forward from this guide, carry with you the understanding that LinkedIn is a tool that evolves with you. Continuously hone your profile, engage with content and connections, and stay abreast of industry trends. Your career is a journey, and LinkedIn is a compass that guides you through its ever-changing terrain. Embrace it as a partner in your professional growth, and you'll unlock doors to opportunities you never knew existed.

Glossary

LinkedIn Profile: Your digital resume showcasing professional experience, skills, and education.

Connection: Other LinkedIn members you choose to connect with are analogous to a 'friend' on social media.

Endorsement: A LinkedIn feature allowing connections to verify your skills.

Recommendation: Written testimonials from LinkedIn connections vouching for your professional abilities.

InMail: LinkedIn's messaging feature allows you to contact connections or others directly.

Networking: Building and maintaining professional relationships beneficial to career growth.

LinkedIn Groups: Online forums within LinkedIn for sharing content and ideas with like-minded professionals.

Job Alerts: Notifications about new job postings relevant to your skills and preferences.

Advanced Search: A LinkedIn tool for refining search results for jobs, people, companies, and more.

Content Creation: The process of developing and sharing informative and engaging material relevant to your industry.

LinkedIn Learning: An online platform offering courses and learning materials across various domains.

Personal Branding: Crafting and promoting a unique professional image and identity.

LinkedIn Pulse: A feature for publishing articles and sharing insights on industry trends.

Algorithm: The system LinkedIn uses to rank and display content and profiles.

Company Page: A LinkedIn page dedicated to a specific company, where they can post updates and job openings.

Engagement: Interaction with content on LinkedIn, including likes, comments, and shares.

Hashtags: Words or phrases prefixed with a '#' to categorize content and enhance discoverability.

Profile Optimization: Enhancing your LinkedIn profile for better visibility and appeal to potential employers or clients.

Skill Assessments: Tests offered by LinkedIn to validate your skills.

Recruiter Profile: A specialized LinkedIn account type used by recruiters and hiring managers.

Salary Insights: Information on salary ranges and compensation trends in various industries and roles.

Open Candidates: A LinkedIn feature that discreetly signals to recruiters that you're open to new opportunities.

LinkedIn Premium: A paid subscription offering additional features like InMail credits, advanced search filters, and more.

Job Market Trends: Current patterns and changes in employment sectors and hiring practices.

Privacy Settings: Controls that manage the visibility of your LinkedIn information and activity.

LinkedIn Influencer: Recognized thought leaders and experts who share insights on the platform.

Network Expansion: Strategies to grow your list of connections on LinkedIn.

SEO (Search Engine Optimization) for LinkedIn: Techniques to enhance your profile's visibility in search results.

Work Anniversary: A LinkedIn feature that celebrates the yearly anniversary of a job position.

Active Status: A LinkedIn feature showing when you or your connections are online.

This glossary will not only clarify terms but also enrich the readers' comprehension of LinkedIn as a multifaceted platform for professional development. It will be an invaluable tool that readers may use to get through your book and their personal LinkedIn experiences.

About the Author

The author of this work for three decades has worked as Marketing Director in a variety of companies operating in the BTB Distribution of products and services in the vast IT landscape, helping to bring one of these companies to life by taking on the role of CEO.

However, his story goes far beyond the mere confines of the professional sphere.

In fact, in parallel with his tireless efforts in business, he has ardently embraced an esoteric path, becoming a Sannyasin, a devoted follower of the visionary spiritual philosopher Osho. This path of soul-searching sharpened his understanding of life, love, and awareness, opening the door to deeper dimensions of human existence.

Many years of his life were devoted to meditative practice in many forms, with a particular affection for shamanism, an ancient way of connecting with nature and the spiritual world. As a "pipe bearer," he was the keeper of a sacred pipe, sharing it in the various rituals celebrated around the fire, thus symbolizing his deep connection with tradition and spirituality.

The author also officiated at numerous ceremonies inside sweat lodges, sharing with others his deep reverence for the wisdom enshrined in these ancient rituals and his deep connection with nature.

With extraordinary skill, the author blends the richness of experience in the business world with a deep understanding of spirituality and mindfulness, offering readers a unique and enriching perspective within this work.

SW Prem Jaganu

As an editor, every single review is a crucial support for me. Your voice can make a difference and help me move forward with my work.

If you believe in the value of what I do and want to help me, please take a moment to share your thoughts.

Your honest and sincere review will be a great help to me, and I will read it very carefully.

I thank you from the bottom of my heart for your valuable contribution.

amzn.to/3uYpFld

APPENDIX BONUS 1

Detailed Guide to Setting Privacy Parameters on LinkedIn

Welcome to the detailed guide on setting up your LinkedIn privacy. This section is crafted to be a valuable help, providing step-by-step instructions on customizing privacy settings. Even if you need to be more tech-savvy, this guide will help you navigate LinkedIn's privacy features with ease.

Understanding LinkedIn Privacy Settings

You can manage your data, exchange information, and decide what others may view about you with LinkedIn's range of privacy settings. These settings are crucial for maintaining a balance between being visible to potential opportunities and protecting your personal information.

Accessing Your Privacy Settings

1. Log into LinkedIn: Start by signing into your LinkedIn account.

2. Go to Settings: In the upper right corner, click on your profile image, then choose "Settings & Privacy."

Key Privacy Settings to Adjust

Profile Viewing Options

- How others see your LinkedIn activity: Choose how your profile appears when you've viewed other profiles. You can be fully visible, semi-anonymous, or completely anonymous.

- Application: Go to the 'Visibility' section and select 'Profile viewing options.'

- Profile Visibility on LinkedIn

- Edit your public profile: Control how your profile looks to non-LinkedIn members and search engines.
- Application: Under 'Visibility,' click on 'Edit your public profile.'

Managing Your Connections

- Who can see your connections: Decide if only you or your connections can see your LinkedIn network. This is useful for maintaining privacy over who you're connected with.
- Application: Find this under 'Visibility of your LinkedIn activity.'

Data Sharing and Privacy

- Data sharing with third-party applications: Control whether LinkedIn can share your data with third-party applications and services.
- Job application settings: Adjust settings for job applications, including saving job application answers.
- Application: These options are located under the 'Data privacy' section.

Communication Preferences

- Who can reach you: Set preferences for who can send you invitations and messages. This is crucial for managing the types of communication you receive.
- Application: Find this under the 'Communications' tab.

Blocking and Hiding

- Blocking and hiding: This feature allows you to block certain LinkedIn members or hide specific posts.
- Application: Located under 'Visibility of your LinkedIn activity.'

Turning Off LinkedIn Activity Broadcasts

- Activity broadcasts: Choose whether to notify your network about profile changes. This is key when you're discreetly updating your profile for job searches.

- Application: This setting is found under 'Visibility of your LinkedIn activity.'

Managing LinkedIn Ad Preferences

- Ad settings: Customize your ad preferences based on interests and information.

- Application: Go to the 'Data privacy' section and select 'Ad settings.'

Regularly Review Your Privacy Settings

It's critical to periodically check and alter your privacy settings, particularly if your professional objectives or job search situation change. LinkedIn revamps its platform frequently, and staying abreast of these changes ensures your privacy preferences are always current.

Conclusion

Your LinkedIn privacy settings are a dynamic tool in your professional toolkit. By understanding and customizing these settings, you empower yourself to control your online professional presence effectively. This guide will help you comfortably and securely take full advantage of this potent platform by guiding you through LinkedIn's privacy landscape.

Remember, the correct privacy settings align with your career objectives while safeguarding your personal information, creating a balanced and productive LinkedIn experience.

APPENDIX BONUS 2

Mastering LinkedIn's Advanced Search and Filters for Efficient Job Hunting

In the digital landscape of job hunting, LinkedIn's advanced search and filters emerge as powerful tools, enabling you to pinpoint job opportunities that align perfectly with your career aspirations. This section delves into the intricate details of using LinkedIn's advanced search features, guiding you to optimize your job search process effectively.

Understanding LinkedIn's Advanced Search

LinkedIn's advanced search feature is a gateway to customizing your job search, ensuring that you encounter opportunities most relevant to your skills and career goals. To access this feature, start on the LinkedIn homepage and navigate to the search bar at the top.

Keywords: Begin with keywords. These can include job titles, skills, companies, or industries. Use quotations for exact phrases, such as "software engineer" or "digital marketing manager."

Filters: Once your keywords have been entered, click the search icon. Next, use the provided filters to refine your results further. These filters are crucial in tailoring your search to specific requirements.

Leveraging Filters for Precision

Location: Specify the geographic area where you're looking for opportunities. You can be as broad as a country or as specific as a city.

Connections: Filter by 1st, 2nd, or 3rd+ degree connections. This is particularly useful if you want to leverage your network in your job search.

Current Companies: If you aim to work for specific companies, use this filter to narrow down job postings from those organizations.

Past Companies: Useful if you want to reconnect with a previous employer or seek opportunities in familiar corporate cultures.

Industries: This filter helps you focus on specific sectors, such as Information Technology, Finance, or Healthcare.

Experience Level: Cater your search to positions that match your expertise, whether entry-level, mid-level, or executive.

Job Function: This allows you to search for roles in specific functions like Marketing, Sales, or Engineering.

Job Type: Select from Full-time, Part-time, Internship, etc., according to the nature of employment you seek.

Date Posted: Use this to find the most recent postings. Options range from 'Past 24 hours' to 'Past Month.'

Salary: Some listings include salary information, enabling you to search for jobs within your desired pay range.

Using Advanced Search to Streamline Job Hunting

Save Searches: Once you've tailored your search, save it to quickly access similar job listings in the future.

Set Alerts: Activate job alerts for your search criteria to receive notifications when new jobs that match your preferences are posted.

Explore 'Open to Work': If you are open to new opportunities, consider adding the 'Open To Work' feature to your profile to indicate your status to recruiters.

Review and Revise: Regularly revisit and adjust your search criteria. As your career goals evolve, so should your job search strategy.

Engage with Listings: Don't just apply; engage with job postings. Commenting or asking insightful questions can make you stand out.

Remember, LinkedIn's advanced search is more than just a job search tool; it's a platform for exploring the vast landscape of professional opportunities. By mastering these search techniques and filters, you can streamline your job search process, saving time and focusing your efforts on the opportunities that truly resonate with your career goals. This efficient approach to job hunting on LinkedIn is an indispensable skill in the modern job market.

APPENDIX BONUS 3

Creating a Comprehensive LinkedIn Profile that Reflects Your Professional Journey

A well-crafted LinkedIn profile is a pivotal tool in your professional toolkit. It's your digital handshake and a powerful way to tell your professional story. Here's a step-by-step guide to creating a profile that resonates with clarity and precision:

Professional Photo and Background Image: Start with a professional headshot. This doesn't mean a stiff corporate photo but one that conveys your professionalism and approachability. The background image should complement your personal brand, whether it's a snapshot of your workspace, an industry-related image, or something that reflects your professional ethos.

Compelling Headline: Your headline should include more than just your job title. Instead, it should encapsulate your professional identity. Think of it as a mini-pitch: "Marketing Specialist at XYZ | Helping Brands Build Engaging Digital Campaigns" is more impactful than just "Marketing Specialist."

Personalized Summary: Your summary is where your story unfolds. This is your opportunity to humanize your profile. Talk about your professional journey, key skills, achievements, and what drives you in your career. Keep it engaging and authentic, and don't be afraid to let your personality shine through.

Detailed Experience Section: List your professional experiences in reverse chronological order. For each role, include a brief description of your responsibilities and significant achievements. Use bullet points for readability and incorporate quantifiable results to validate your accomplishments.

Education and Certifications: Add your educational background, including any relevant courses or certifications that enhance your professional standing. This section provides more context about your knowledge base and expertise.

Skills and Endorsements: Populate the skills section with relevant skills and regularly update it. Encourage colleagues to endorse your skills, as these serve as quick testimonials of your abilities.

Recommendations: Personal recommendations add credibility. Politely ask former or current colleagues, clients, or supervisors for recommendations that highlight your strengths and working style.

Accomplishments and Projects: Include any significant projects, publications, languages, patents, or honors and awards. This section adds depth to your profile and showcases a well-rounded professional.

Customized URL: Personalize your LinkedIn URL to make it clean and shareable. A URL with your name is more professional and more accessible to remember.

Engaging with Content: Regularly post, share, and comment on articles relevant to your industry. This not only shows that you're up to date with your field but also increases your visibility on the platform.

Privacy Settings: Familiarize yourself with LinkedIn's privacy settings to control what is visible on your profile and to whom. Tailor these settings according to your comfort and professional goals.

Profile Completeness: LinkedIn guides you through the process of completing your profile. Aim for the "All-Star" level to ensure maximum visibility.

Creating a comprehensive LinkedIn profile is an ongoing process. Update your profile frequently to reflect newly acquired knowledge, accomplishments, and experiences. This living document serves as your professional narrative to the world, telling your story with clarity and precision and opening doors to new opportunities.

APPENDIX BONUS 4

LinkedIn Salary Tool: Your Guide to Understanding Potential Earnings

In today's competitive job market, understanding potential earnings is crucial. LinkedIn's Salary Tool is designed to offer a comprehensive view of salary expectations across various roles and sectors. Here's a detailed guide to using this tool effectively:

Accessing the LinkedIn Salary Tool

Navigation: Access the LinkedIn Salary Tool either directly through the LinkedIn Salary website or by navigating to the 'Jobs' tab on LinkedIn and selecting 'Salary' from the menu.

Search Functionality: Once on the LinkedIn Salary page, you'll find a search bar. Here, you can enter a job title and, optionally, a location to begin your salary exploration.

Understanding Salary Data

Salary Ranges: The tool displays a range of salaries for the specified position. This range includes the lower, median, and upper salary limits, giving a clear picture of potential earnings.

Base Pay and Additional Compensation: LinkedIn divides the salary data into base pay and additional compensation. Base pay refers to the fixed income before bonuses or other benefits. Further compensation includes bonuses, commissions, and other financial benefits, offering a holistic view of total potential earnings.

Data Source: LinkedIn's salary data is crowdsourced from its users. Professionals anonymously submit their salary information, ensuring a diverse and realistic data pool.

Personalized Insights

Filters for Customization: To tailor the information, LinkedIn provides filters such as years of experience, education level, company size, and industry. These filters help in narrowing down the data to match your specific background or career aspirations.

Location-based Data: Salary expectations vary by location due to cost of living and demand differences. LinkedIn's tool allows you to compare salaries in different cities or regions, which is particularly helpful for those considering relocation.

Comparative Analysis: The tool also enables users to compare different job titles or industries side by side. This feature is beneficial for those contemplating a career change or progression.

Confidentiality and Reliability

Anonymity: Users provide their salary information anonymously. This ensures privacy and encourages more users to share their data, leading to a more comprehensive database.

Data Verification: LinkedIn employs various methods to verify and validate the data, ensuring its accuracy and reliability.

Utilizing the Tool for Career Advancement

Negotiation Leverage: Understanding the market rate for a role provides leverage in salary negotiations, ensuring you're not undervaluing yourself.

Career Planning: Insights from the tool can guide your career decisions, helping you understand which roles, industries, or locations offer better financial prospects.

Professional Development: By identifying the skills and qualifications that impact salaries in your field, you can strategically plan your professional development.

In conclusion, LinkedIn's Salary Tool is a powerful resource for gaining insight into potential earnings across various professions. By providing detailed salary ranges, additional compensation details, and personalized filters, it equips professionals with the necessary information to make informed career choices, negotiate effectively, and align their career trajectories with financial goals.

APPENDIX BONUS 5

Understanding LinkedIn Learning

LinkedIn Learning is a vital part of the LinkedIn ecosystem, providing individuals with an online learning environment to enhance their professional knowledge and skills. This in-depth manual will explore LinkedIn Learning in detail and offer advice on how to make the most of it for both personal and professional development.

1. What is LinkedIn Learning? LinkedIn Learning is an extension of LinkedIn, the world's largest professional network. With regard to business, technology, and creative skills, among other subjects, it provides customers with access to an extensive library of video courses. These courses, which professionals in the subject teach, are intended to be interesting, educational, and immediately applicable to a range of professional domains.

2. Course Offerings and Structure: the platform boasts thousands of courses, ranging from short tutorials to more comprehensive learning paths. Courses are structured into bite-sized videos, making them easy to consume and convenient for busy professionals. Each course is typically accompanied by downloadable resources, quizzes, and practice exercises to reinforce learning.

3. Personalized Learning Experience: one of LinkedIn Learning's standout features is its customized course recommendations. The platform uses data from your LinkedIn profile, such as your job title, skills, and industry, to suggest relevant courses. This ensures that the learning content is aligned with your professional goals and the demands of your industry.

4. Integration with LinkedIn Profile: upon completing a course, learners have the option to add these skills to their LinkedIn profiles. This feature not only keeps your profile current but also communicates your dedication to lifelong learning to contacts in your network and prospective employers.

5. **Learning Paths for Career Advancement: LinkedIn Learning offers curated learning paths for specific career roles or skill development. These paths are a series of courses designed to provide in-depth learning on a particular subject, helping professionals to prepare for the next step in their careers or to delve into new areas of interest.

6. **Staying Current with Industry Trends: the platform is continuously updated with new courses, ensuring content remains relevant in the face of rapidly evolving industry standards and practices. It's an excellent resource for staying informed about the latest trends and technologies in your field.

7. **Flexibility and Accessibility: courses on LinkedIn Learning are accessible anytime and anywhere and are compatible with desktop and mobile devices. This flexibility allows learners to engage with content at their own pace and on their own schedule, making it ideal for professionals balancing work and personal commitments.

8. **Certificates of Completion: Learners obtain a certificate of completion upon finishing a course or learning route. You can further establish your professional credibility by sharing these certifications with your network and adding them to your LinkedIn page.

9. **Benefits for Job Seekers: LinkedIn Learning provides courses that assist in building abilities that employers highly value for job seekers looking for new chances. It also helps in preparing for job interviews and improving job-hunting strategies.

10. **Subscription Model: LinkedIn Learning operates on a subscription model, offering access to all its courses and materials for a monthly or annual fee. However, many organizations provide free access to LinkedIn Learning through corporate or educational partnerships.

Conclusion: in essence, LinkedIn Learning is a dynamic, user-friendly platform ideal for professionals aiming to enhance their skills, stay competitive in their industry, and advance their careers. Its integration with LinkedIn's professional network further amplifies its value, making it a key tool for personal and professional development in today's fast-paced job market.

Made in the USA
Coppell, TX
01 January 2025

43792053R00049